The Untold Butterfly

A collection of Life hacks to connecting poems

Margaret Wanjiku Ndiritu

Made with ❤ on the BookLeaf Publishing Platform
www.bookleafpub.in
www.bookleafpub.com

Dedication

Cherishing the adventurous trips I've taken.
Surrendering to the most high, giving in and connected
with the universe . This is bringing so much joy and
poetry to share, it's been a humbling experience learning
myself deeper and growing everyday on becoming a
better mother of two beautiful children. My love bugs

Preface

Acknowledgements

1. Yo Energy!

Yo mama got energy, she keeps up with me
Angel right on my phone. In disbelief
A new research study for my new project
Body wrapped with milk chocolate drip
Push thru with an exotic essence to dare
Bonita! She speak my language
Simple her flow, can't no other compare
So complex and yet so clumsy make her cute
His money talk but she no listen
Come now let me put on my best
So intrigued, too good to walk away
Bilingual to bullshit, can't control her
Best she knows what to do
That's my baby yo, can't complain
we vibin
To force is pressure, unravel my heart
He detects her like smelling weed
All eyes on her, No blinking, to never miss a moment
It's a new day and yet still blessed
She's still in my life, never quit
Holy Ghost fire, super natural feels
Boost my confidence, give me happiness
like a nice song, can't wait for the remix
Our love will last forever, content

I can feel you, i can see you
You amazing girl i love you
my heart desire
my true lover

2. The Tango

You come around once in a life time
Giving such enticement, start glowing
Can't look you in your eye too long
Scared i might fall for you fast
Leaving me pondering about what's next
Them butterfly feelings are real
Being spontaneous my mind be puzzled
To me you are one of a kind, Unique
Bringing in dilemma, i need yah
To some it come as a surprise
But to me God answered my prayers
Quick to my crafty ways, you know
Never a dull moment, we entice
Giving that back and forth like see-saw
When i touch you, i get chills
Got that vibe that don't let up
Having comeback that never disappoint
All in all you do it for me
Keep me close, I'll keep you warm
You satisfy me in more than one way
Baby give me that affection, I embrace
See what you didn't see me coming
But i come in peace to love and cherish
don't get it twisted, i can stand alone

But with you, time fly by
In the midst of feelings, i engage
Let's Tango

3. My Motto

I don't want to wait till your
gone
All i want is you now and forever
They don't get me like you do
The way you finish my thoughts
Triggering me to act accordingly
Haven't had this feeling in a
while
The go thing is hard but i have
you
I know it might just sound like
words
But i write from my soul
Would never say what i don't

mean

Keeping in 100% is the code
decoded

I like knowing your thinking
about me

One of a kind, Rare than an
eclipse

You shower me with your ideas

In that makes me wanna do
better

Ambitious man be my superman

Give or take I'll never let go

My motto if you smart you will
never leave

We cater to each other,
cherishing us

Having growth and adventure

Making better memories

Cheers to life with no judgement

just live

4. Care

In the time of despair, you
wonder
Taking in all emotions at hand
C'mon now i've done better in
life for this
To happen in such a way it
shocketh
Now how to recollect and move
on
My love, for the world dwindles
Hanging on, having hope so
crusial
I keep thinking, It's like a roller
coaster

There's a rise after a fall, a silver
lining
Knowing the sun is rising
tomorrow
There's always a chance for
another try
Another moment with different
results
I must and will continue to
inspire
The only one i need to believe in
is God and me
One of the best time in life is
when you meet another
Praying the journey gets easier
it does change, but now what's

different
A hug at the end of the day
A kiss to forget all else
It's those moments we keep
striving for
In despair you find comfort in
another
Embracing self and others having
empathy
We bless each other to grow
Make it a team effort to live this
life
Boy would it be easier if we just
Care

5. I'm not like your last

Look here i may be a tease
I thought that was the game
To keep you hanging on wanting
more
I don't wanna over do it
I don't want to be like your last
I want to be the last
Becoming what you need
Seeing you point of view
i don't wanna waste time either
I want you to know my heart
I fucking wolf you
Don't let go, time is coming
The wait worth it all and then

some
Never changed on you, Except
for growth
I got options but im opting you
You fir like a glove, Guilty
Making me come out of my shell
Vulnerable times you never make
fun
Your like what my heart warms
to
Be done and be mine

6. They Not Like Us

It be the discovering stages that
trigger
Not knowing what a person
brings to the table
You start learning their patterns
and habits
Looking for any red flags that
carry weight
Bulls eye to the blue print, we
escaped
They not like us, we tried
different
All in or nothing it felt like, so
glazing

I'm lowkey satisfied, easy
breathing
Like Tupac and Jeda, we went
there
Unraveling every emotion with
care
Made up for one heck of a year
Is it possible? Yes i think so
To be different, to become the
elite
That dared to see different

7. The Let Go

To forgive is not to forget
In moments i see a different light
A time to celebrate what's here
Than dwell over spilled milk
Moments when one satisfies thier
inner child
Cherish what is at hand
My mama always said just let it
go
I never wanted to agree, i wanted
justice
Yes i found that in the most high
i let go of the wheel and said
Jesus take control

It be them moments i beg for
peace

To recollect and savor what is
here

looking forward with positive
vibrations

It's a hard potato to swallow
sometimes

But moving on is needed for
healing

Do i want to punch a hole in the
wall

Maybe so now i have a broken
hand

Self care starts with you, so
what's next?

Giving less fucks and doing you!
The let go of false thinking about
how to love
we accept first then love
The let go brings faith for the
future

8. She Ain't No Runner

Been ahead of my game
They call me the trendsetter
See i saw beyond the maze
Over taking the huddles and
progressing
Accepting who i am and
conforming
I began digging in deep in my
soul for more
Oh what a journey it becomes
Always simple whispers to
inspire
I wish i could have known sooner
That i needed to find him

Just as much as he was looking
for me
Learning lessons that changed
my direction
Not giving up but giving in to the
most high
Played my cards right and got
blessed
So playful with the words
Lets entice

9. Not Enough Time

I keep stepping even though of
the step backs
Literally living one day at a time
Praying for a peaceful productive
day
Just because i feel like there's
more to me
For me to be feeling excited to
share
Overcoming my deepest fears
and letting go
Misunderstood to the mass but
let me explain
i come with exciting ideas

Do i have enough time to tell my
story
Mapping out my life see magic
Holding on to faith of a mustard
seed
i'm the unicorn that manifested
I want more from this life, leave a
legacy
Expecting the unexpected
Being at the right place and the
right time
Real intense moments, that
shook me up
Dealing with people that have
less care
Sprinkle sprinkle, the magic dust

in the air

Deserve to live a life of magic

So many untold stories

Let's dive in and explore

10. Extra

Everything is intentional
It's like i trust myself
Having this pleasure to express
Giving forth what is real
Keeping it classy with the grace
walk
Cut out all negative vibes
Let's rock and roll the emotions
rolling
Come at me for clarity
The glow up became the come up
Basic thinking they had about
the flow
Now ready to elaborate what was

mistaken

Lead with good intentions and
keeping your eye on the prize
And Being Extra

11. The unknown

The unknown is calling
Waiting to be discovered
I paid attention to you
Learning what makes you tick
Never crossing the line
Trying to make it forever
Never a dull moment
That back and forth moments
To make new memories
We had to accept each other
Build a bond undeniable
Never doing to much
Giving a second thought
Looking inward and opening up

Becoming vulnerable with
another
Making cherishable memories
Together the unknown is the
grey are to make better

12. Pure Reasoning

Baby are you ok?

No I'm Good, Just want it my
way

Like the president, control of the
whole world

What if i called the shots, so
gracefully

A lot of power for a girl i know
that's real

It's just progress takes change

Wanted everyone to be able to
visit any country for cheap

Enabling connection all the way
thru

Having all the resources making
it great
The point is your free to explore
Go to Britain next weekend your
in Dubai
To where we really have no
country
So many rules to follow and for
what
Yes structure rules but can cut off
dictatorship
The greed that separated the
world
More growth are the ones that
live in peace

13. Show Love

It's always about those courting
moments
When you looking at self and
realizing
You really might be in love with
this person
Catching yourself doing things
you wouldn't do
Praying and hoping they see you
You do things to make him proud
Forming a relation that means a
whole lot
Heart skipping a beat everytime
you speak

My inner child healing revealing
prince charming
How you move with mystery,
enticing
We have so much time to role
play
Show this man i'm worth his
time
New energy needed, creating
new life
surrendering to your energy we
ignite
Love so tender, fluffy feels to
entice
rejuvinating my life and soul

14. Get Silly

Better attitude
Make yeah feel the funtitude
Give in a bit and have gratitude
Diving deep to catch them
feelings
In a magnitude of chaos
I declare my love to my baby boo
He always come in crunch gotta
love that
From the first time we met I
knew
Something that lead him coming
back
It's the same thing that fires my

passion

It be the little things foreal

So amazing how he love me so

Never let go of something so
amazing

So dedicated I am to his
demeanor

Nothing is stopping us in going
places

My pleasure to always do for me

Every second is a new beginning

Sweetest love there is

15. Limit

I was made to hbe limitless
A fighter, went thru the struggles
All watching me to fall off foreal
Try coming back from my
struggles
So positive, help inspire others
Learning how to trust the most
high
Surrendering and leading by faith
Purifying my slate, new me, new
life
Visualization and manifestation
I create my own reality, striving
Having i am worth it attitude

Ready for battle, Trigger happy
Not scared to go ham for Jesus
in the pits, i learned my enemy
I provide and protect us if i could
so i learned the truth, the blue
print
Out of the matrix, let it go,
control
Doing my shadow work,
Acceptance
I learned grew and now i share
I am fully in my power
Making room for growth
Being Limiteless

16. Come On

You should have never done that
All you did was made you known
For the hypocrite you became
Jealousy growing like hate
Looking at me like a wishful
fulfillment
Wanting my blessing you tried to
steal
But i know the justice giver
Transmuted my pain into
purpose
I took care of me that much more
thru thick and thin i looked

inward

emotionally in control, return to
sender

Been knocked around, learned
my lesson

Standing on business, Bull's eye
to the gold

You come for me

 i show you the business

17. Apex Affect

Now i am at my wits end
Real story happening live
Just got kicked out of my home
While i was in the process of
writing my book
With barely any options of places
to go
I still hold on knowing God will
make a way
I'm scared God
I know you got me
So much to pack
The owners wanted us to move
pronto

Never cared to really know me

But yet had so much negative to

say about you

 I got back on my drawing board

Asking self, My freedom or

another cell

Being grounded to reality

Just being in Limbo with not a

sole near

Karma never tasted so sweet

So i reclaim my energy and pray

18. Focus

The fear of missing out
But when you chase God
He shall add all things to your
life
Chasing to another level and
elevating
Accepting what God has in store
The best is yet to come, Amen!
Excited about your growth in the
kingdom
Super natural, extra ordinary
blessings
because you chose to believe in
jesus

it takes another level of
preparation
some days you may be down
But this narrow path is not by
yourself
Talk to Jesus, to lead you
The father has spoken to your
heart
You done ran for long enough
Make it you time to rise and
praise
The lord has an assignment for
you
The blue print is with you, use it
Manifested in the physical and
receiving

Knowing there's brighter days to
come
Focus evaluating change
Becoming more of yourself

19. Know about me

Quick to pick up the pen
Always the popular loner
Intended to see me
But this is divine timing
I'm in a different place
Everyday i find more of my
mantel
To be the original of something
it has to grow to be worth it
Only time would really tell
My children , make is all worth it
This writing thing had been the
string i"ve been holding on to
I'm on a journey the wilderness

don't scare me

Stand confident and strive

Go get that food lioness

20. This mission

They judge you unrighteously
Now realizing who i am
Waiting me to entertain the
devil
We ain't going backwards, we
know better
Smoking mirrors have been
cleared
Tower hitting left to right
Karma never misses it's target
Focused on the mission is a
passion
Be ware don't let the past back
More darma coming my way

Speaking the truth and wisdom
How i move on, i am releasing
grudges
Curse breaker , Soul changer
On a mission
 i give my self closure
I give my self power

21. The Affect

Now i give my prayers into the
cosmic
Protecting my peace and energy
Knowing that i am never alone
I plead you hear this words with
intent
Be the change you wanted to see
For seeing the next couple of
weeks will be tough
Your are needed on this earth i
keep telling self
I keep turning my eye to the evil
i see
Praying not to be influenced but

used by God

Now i set forth and have given
my all

I pray this book buy me a home
to write more

Enjoy the rollercoaster ride and
let one have a different out put

Chea